European Foundation for the Improvement of Living and Working Conditions

A programme for 1997 – 2000

Facing up to the challenges of European society

Wyattville Road,
Loughlinstown,
Co. Dublin, Ireland
Tel: +353 1 204 3100
Fax: +353 1 282 6456

Cataloguing data can be found at the end of this publication

Luxembourg: Office for Official Publications of the European Communities, 1996

ISBN 92-827-8593-9

Printed in Ireland

Preface

Every four years, in preparing its Rolling Programme, the European Foundation for the Improvement of Living and Working Conditions has an opportunity to review its strategy and the orientation to be given to its activities and in particular its research projects.

The present 1997-2000 programme is essentially the outcome of detailed discussions within and between the groups making up the Administrative Board of the Foundation, representing government, employer organizations and worker organizations in Member States as well as the European Commission. Contacts and exchanges were also organized with representatives of other EU institutions and bodies.

In accordance with the Regulation governing the European Foundation for the Improvement of Living and Working Conditions, the Foundation's management has taken account of the views of the Committee of Experts, expressed during a meeting on 17 and 18 June 1996.

Following a joint meeting on 12 September 1996 of members of the Administrative Board and of the Committee of Experts, the Four-Year Rolling Programme 1997-2000 was approved by the Administrative Board at its meeting of 13 September 1996, in Dublin. It provides the framework within which the Foundation's annual programmes of work will be defined on an annual basis, from 1997 to 2000.

Clive Purkiss, Director

Eric Verborgh, Deputy Director

Dublin, September 1996

Contents

CHAPTER 1   Introduction

In framing its sixth four-year rolling programme, the Foundation recognises that Europe is experiencing a period of profound social and economic change. The European Union needs to respond to a whole series of challenges, the cumulative effect of which poses a severe threat to the achievement of its social goals:

... *"to promote throughout the Community a harmonious and balanced development of economic activities, sustainable and non-inflationary growth respecting the environment, a high degree of convergence of economic performance, a high level of employment and of social protection, the raising of the standard of living and quality of life, and economic and social cohesion and solidarity among its Member States".* (Article G(2) of the Treaty on European Union, 1992).

These shared goals reflect a broad consensus on the kind of society to which the Member States jointly aspire and much has already been achieved. However the globalization of trade and production, the growing impact of the information society, demographic and structural change and the persistently high level of unemployment are all combining to put unprecedented pressure on the economic and social structure of the Union.

It is in this context that the Foundation has re-examined its role and the contribution it can make to the planning and establishment of better living and working conditions in Europe.

The Role of the Foundation

Over twenty years of experience, the Foundation has forged for itself a specific role in the improvement of the quality of life in the European Union. Through the management and analysis of research and information, the Foundation provides decision-makers in Europe with knowledge to assist them in responding to the challenges society is facing. At the centre of a network which actively engages the key actors – European and national government policy-makers; employer and trade union representative organizations; voluntary and community organizations; and researchers – the Foundation's work is characterised by the innovative nature of its studies and critical analyses of the major factors influencing change in society. It aims to identify priorities for action to improve the living and working conditions of European citizens, through comparative work and in the light of practical and concrete experience, looking to the medium and long-term future.

The Foundation offers added value in its role of research and information provider, from its close involvement with the key social actors and by using an integrated and holistic approach to living and working conditions. Thus the Foundation has developed an approach which encompasses consideration of the relevant economic, social and environmental dimensions of societal change in an active exchange and development of knowledge. The complexity of the challenges facing the European Union dictates such a comprehensive approach and demands the development of a multi-faceted response. In this way the Foundation aims to build understanding of the key issues and to put forward options and advice for policy-making.

Over the years the Foundation has extended its research methods and techniques of information collection, as well as its publication and dissemination practices. Such continuous development has enabled the Foundation substantially to expand the range and impact of its activities and adapt them to the changing needs of its audiences.

The missions of the Foundation

The Regulation establishing the Foundation, Regulation (EEC) No 1365/75 of the Council (OJ No L 139 of 30.5.1975), states that its aim "shall be to contribute to the planning and establishment of better living and working conditions through action designed to increase and disseminate knowledge likely to assist this development" (Article 2.1). This defines not only the Foundation's *research* aim but also its role as a body *disseminating* knowledge, as required by its Regulation, which specifies that the Foundation "shall take the relevant Community policies into account when carrying out its tasks. It shall advise the Community institutions on foreseeable objectives and guidelines by forwarding in particular scientific information and technical data" (Article 2.2).

The preamble setting forth the reasons for this Regulation points out that "the problems presented by the improvement of living and working conditions in modern society are increasingly numerous and complex"; and that "it is important that appropriate Community action should be built up on an inter-disciplinary scientific basis and at the same time that employers and workers should be associated in the action undertaken". The structure of the Foundation (employers' organizations, employees' organizations, governments of the Member States, European Commission) reflects its partnership approach to the development of its work programmes and its priorities, and enables a close involvement of these actors in the dissemination and debate of the results of the Foundation's work.

The *production*, *discussion* and *dissemination* of information are thus the key elements around which the Foundation's activities are built.

Towards a 1997-2000 Programme for the Foundation

Changes in European society set the context for the identification and implementation of the main activities in the new work programme. The European social model is built on two main foundations: full employment and social solidarity, although these were not universally achieved. They are both now facing severe crises, putting a severe strain on Europe's ability to continue to build a solidair, creative, productive and thus competitive society in a wide sense. The globalization of markets is bringing continued structural change with a need to improve competitiveness, innovative capacity and efficiency. The need for action on unemployment is especially pressing, both for the millions seeking work and for maintaining the solidarity of society as a whole. Significant demographic changes are underway, seen in population ageing and population mobility as well as in changing family structures, which are a reflection of deeper structural changes in society. New technologies, pressures on the environment and the development of the Information Society are demanding a European debate on how our patterns of life and work should be changed so as to preserve the strong hold of Europe: participation and social dialogue. The main players in these processes of change – governments, employers, trade unions – have to examine new strategies to address these changes, new allocations of responsibility, new roles and partnerships, new forms of cooperation and solidarity. The Foundation has to help the main players by developing visions on how to face up the main challenges and how to address them in such a way that burdens are shared equally by all parts of society and that sustainable development of our societies is guaranteed.

A number of other key developments will affect the scope and content of the Foundation's contribution in the coming years. Policy developments at the European level (Economic and Monetary Union; the Inter-Governmental Conference and its outcomes; enlargement of the Union) will impact on both the *context* of the Foundation's work and on its *mission* (new tasks as proposed by the European Council in 1993; more direct collaboration with the services of the European Commission; cooperation with CEDEFOP and other newly-established agencies such as those for Safety and Health at Work (Bilbao) and for the Environment (Copenhagen), as well as the European Centre for Industrial Relations (Florence)). From its *experience* built on twenty years of research and active exchange of knowledge in the area of living and working conditions, the Foundation is particularly well placed to contribute to the reflection and debate on the challenges facing European society:

❑ **employment**

❑ **equal opportunities**

❑ **health and well-being**

❑ **sustainable development**

❑ **social cohesion**

❑ **participation.**

As regards *employment,* unemployment and a retreat from solidarity have been clearly signalled as the two greatest threats to the kind of society which is the goal of the European Union. Work is a central value in European society. Despite continuing economic growth, nearly twenty million unemployed people continue to bear witness to the scale of the challenge to provide employment for those who require it. The content and duration of work has also been changing under pressures to improve labour market efficiency and long-run competitiveness. There is a growing need to provide good quality, skilled and stable jobs, accessible also to those who are at present excluded. *Equal opportunities* is a core objective in this process, particularly between men and women but also for those, who for reasons of age, ethnicity, health, disability, religion, sexual orientation or other factors, are excluded from full participation in working life or in society in general.

The maintenance and promotion of *health and well-being* are key elements in improving the quality of life, equal opportunities and social cohesion. Particular efforts must continue to be made to ensure good health for all those at work. As more of Europe's population is pushed to the margins (50 million poor people in the EU), there are considerable problems preventing social protection systems from finding the resources required to guarantee a satisfactory quality of life for all and equal access to opportunities for participation and development. This brings an increased challenge to *social cohesion* and the building of a Europe based on solidarity, rights and responsibilities.

Participation and the development of a more active and inclusive society are issues of growing significance and debate. Democracy is a central value in European society, but social and economic trends have also influenced the desire for more involvement of a better educated and informed population as well as those who are disadvantaged. Significant changes are underway at the workplace and in industrial relations as well as in political life. The concept of European citizenship and what this might mean in terms of rights and responsibilities is on the agenda and efforts are being made to involve those on the margins in the development of social policies.

Economic development which is more job intensive must be the key to meeting these challenges but, as is clearly recognised, this *development* must be environmentally friendly and *sustainable.* Recent reports by the Commission on the implementation of its current action programme on the environment and sustainable development and by the European Environment Agency on the state of the environment concluded that action taken in the EU to date is insufficient to lead to full integration of environmental considerations into economic sectors, or to sustainable and socially inclusive development.

The responses that are required to meet these multiple and interconnected challenges will require a co-operative partnership between the European Institutions, the Member State governments, the organizations of the social partners and of European citizens. Achieving a Europe of opportunities for all requires both competitiveness and social progress. The key resource will be a well-educated, highly motivated and adaptable population, with high levels of social solidarity. An important tool for policy development will be the availability of adequate data and analyses of the changing situation and of the options available to society's key actors.

It is in this way, by confronting the challenges of European society, that the Foundation will make its contribution over the next four years and into the next century.

CHAPTER 2 The Challenges

Introduction

This four year rolling programme aims to provide the framework for the development of the Foundation's annual programmes of work from 1997 to 2000, in which its various projects and activities are detailed. In this chapter the six main challenges identified in Chapter 1 are elaborated and the past and future contribution of the Foundation to their understanding is clarified. However, these challenges do not stand as single issues to be approached in isolation. In all its activities – research, debate and dissemination of information – the Foundation will aim not only to set out options and priorities in tackling these challenges, but also explicitly to take account of the intricate relationships and linkages between the key issues.

The need to deal with the challenges in a transversal way will also be taken into account in the Foundation's monitoring and evaluation procedures, with new methods being developed to improve debate and exchange of information with the key audiences of the Foundation's work, within the processes of the work as well as in the delivery of results.

The Foundation can be only one contributor to the complex process of addressing the challenges facing the European Union. Its resources and areas of competence are limited. It must therefore focus on the areas in which it can offer added value because of its expertise or specific structure. It is clear that employment is an issue of central importance and will provide a key focus for the Foundation's future work. The related crisis in the welfare state and threats to social solidarity are also of crucial concern. These issues obviously run across the six challenges the Foundation has identified as priorities for its attention. In addition, the following considerations will be taken into account in assessing proposals for inclusion in the annual programmes of work:

❏ the political relevance of the subject at European level, for governments and for the social partners;

❏ lack of knowledge, particularly of a comparative nature at European level, of the topic in question;

❏ avoiding duplication of work done elsewhere, whilst acknowledging a need for complementarity and collaboration;

❏ the added value that the Foundation's structure offers by involving and encouraging debate between the main actors and in promoting close working relationships;

❏ the areas of competence and expertise of the Foundation, in particular its adoption of an integrated and holistic approach to the analysis of living and working conditions and interactive methods of knowledge development;

11

❏ the need to improve communication and dissemination methods.

In its projects the Foundation will pay particular attention to the need for critical analysis of policy and practice; the need to understand and take account of different geographical settings and regional variations; involving in its work as far as is practical the main social actors, including public authorities, the social partners and the voluntary and community sectors, and the need to develop closer collaboration with the services of the European Commission and of the other European Institutions. The function of the Foundation as a forum for debate between these key players will be reinforced and further developed.

This programme sets out a new approach for the Foundation, which it is believed will enable it to respond effectively to the needs of its audiences. It will require innovative working and dissemination methods, both internally and with other organisations, taking advantage of the Foundation's specific European mandate and the quadripartite structure of its Administrative Board.

Employment

The Challenge

Employment, job creation and the fight against unemployment are widely perceived as priority social challenges in the European Union. Economic growth has not automatically translated into more jobs, and unemployment has remained persistently high.

The structure of the labour market has itself been undergoing considerable change, with increasing flexibility and reductions in working time, increased female participation and a growing proportion of employment in the services area. Between 1970 and 1991 jobs in services grew by an annual 1.4 million and are now the major source of employment in the Union. These jobs are characterised by a high rate of female employment, more part–time working than in other sectors and a high proportion of self-employment and jobs in small businesses.

The labour market increasingly demands high skill and education levels, employers and workers open to lifelong learning, mobility and new ways to work. Total employment in the EU has at best been stable, and the EU employment rate is currently too low. The challenge is for the Union to find a way to meet the need for decent work and income for its population and to remain competitive in a global economy. This has been exposed in the White Paper on "Growth, competitiveness, employment: the challenges and ways forward into the 21st century", the conclusions of the European Council in Essen and the Santer European pact of confidence for employment. To promote the improvement of living and working conditions, particularly the goals of equal opportunities and social solidarity, it will be necessary to broaden access to work, to pay more attention to the quality of work and work environments and to spread income more equitably.

Improving the employment situation will require more effective collaboration and the development of partnerships between the different actors in society and between the European, national and local levels of authority. The Foundation believes that it is in a good position to assist economic and social policy-makers, the social partners and others concerned, in their attempts to create more and better quality jobs. In particular it can help to define the parameters under which technological and structural adjustment, respect for workers' and citizens' rights and the creation of more jobs can be achieved simultaneously, and recognised as equal goals.

Contribution of the Foundation's past and current programmes

The changing conditions of employment, the nature of work and the quality of working life have been a central focus of the Foundation's work since its establishment in the mid-1970s. Increasingly attention has also been paid to developments in working time, non-standard forms of work and work organisation, the implications of rising unemployment, and strategies for tackling unemployment. A theme running through many of the Foundation's studies has been the impact of information technology and the development of the information society.

In recent years, the Foundation has worked in the following areas:

❏ monitoring and analysis of changes in working time and their implications for living and working conditions;

❏ the development of teleworking as an aspect of the Information Society;

❏ the combining of paid employment with other social and family obligations, including the gender dimensions of part-time work; working and caring; changing labour markets and gender roles, and changes in time use patterns;

❏ counselling and adult guidance: its role in a changing labour market and as a means to reduce and prevent long-term unemployment;

❏ the reduction of age barriers to job recruitment and training and the implications of an ageing workforce for working conditions and the work environment;

❏ documentation and analysis of changes in work organisation and working conditions in different employment sectors;

❏ developments in worker participation and industrial relations in the context of a changing labour market;

❏ employment and sustainability, looking at the impact on employment of environment policies and moves towards sustainable development.

The results of these studies have contributed to the ongoing reflection on the future of work in Europe and on the development of an active society.

Future orientation

Employment issues will be a central focus of attention in the forthcoming work of the Foundation. This will prioritise three main themes: the potential for job creation offered through improvements in living and working conditions; improvement in the quality of employment and of working conditions; and the development of improved and more equitable access to good employment opportunities by disadvantaged groups and in disadvantaged regions. The objectives of the Foundation will therefore be:

❏ to identify the impediments and opportunities for employment growth and for the improvement of working conditions and sustainable development, especially in the service sector, and in new and alternative areas of employment;

❑ to assess and analyse the potential offered by increased positive flexibility and changing patterns of life, care, work and learning;

❑ to analyse flexibility in individual and global contexts;

❑ to examine new approaches and working methods in order to increase the involvement of social actors in issues of job creation, increased flexibility and quality of working life.

❑ to improve understanding of the job creation potentials of the social economy and the development of a more active society.

The Foundation's work will take advantage of its close collaboration and working relationships with the social partners in order to improve understanding of the implications of the changing nature of work and the labour market for different groups of citizens (women and men, old and young, disabled, migrants); for different regions of the Union; for different sectors of the economy (public, private, industry, services); and for different occupations, competences and skills. The implications of the Information Society and changing patterns of time use will also be key foci of attention.

Equal opportunities

The Challenge

As the White Paper on European Social Policy confirms, *'the European Union has a long-standing commitment to equal opportunities for women and men'* (COM (94) 333 of 27 July 1994) and it is recognised that the legal framework of social policy in this area has been a catalyst for significant change in the Member States. This commitment to gender equality remains a key objective and is increasingly perceived as a significant factor in realising the full potential of Europe's human resources and achieving greater competitiveness and economic growth. Given the challenges the Union currently faces, the contribution which women can make to the revitalization of the economy and the development of a more active society is seen as an important reason why the issue of equality should be taken into account in all relevant mainstream policies. Despite considerable progress over the last two decades, much remains to be achieved in realising the goal of equal opportunity for men and women.

Recently the debate on equal opportunities has widened to encompass issues of non-discrimination on grounds other than gender. This view has been argued in the Reflection Group's Report on the Inter-Governmental Conference and in the context of the European Social Policy Forum, held in Brussels in March 1996. Equal opportunities as a principle is seen as one of the shared values of European society. It is a concept fundamental to human rights in a democratic society, closely linked to principles of justice and freedom. However, it must also result in changes of practice: in reality there are groups and individuals who suffer direct or indirect discrimination because of age, gender, disability, ethnicity, health, language, nationality, physical appearance, religion, sexual orientation and other reasons.

Inequalities may reveal themselves in differences in treatment in education, housing, health, income or economic and social integration. Some current developments may even be leading to an increase in unequal treatment or opportunities, such as sustained and high levels of unemployment and a real or perceived uncertainty about the economic future. These can lead to further breakdowns in social solidarity, greater mistrust and indifference, unequal treatment, exclusion and even hostility and violence.

Closing the gap between the principle of equal opportunities and its application in practice remains a major challenge and priority goal for the European Union. The Foundation has paid increasing attention to this issue in recent years and it is the stated objective of the Administrative Board not only to develop this area of work in its own right, but to seek to build an equality and gender perspective in all relevant projects and activities.

16

Contribution of the Foundation's past and current programmes

In the area of equal opportunities between women and men, the Foundation has, from its inception, monitored the relevance of its work to achievement of this objective. Following such an assessment in 1992, it was agreed to devote greater attention to issues of direct concern to equal opportunities for women and to consciously seek to mainstream gender issues in all relevant projects. In this context, the following studies and activities have been undertaken:

- ❑ documentation and analysis of collective bargaining on equal opportunities for women and men at work, identifying successful strategies and good practice;

- ❑ the role of women in locally-based citizen action to combat social and economic exclusion;

- ❑ an equal opportunity analysis of initiatives to improve the quality and effectiveness of public welfare services and to develop greater consumer involvement;

- ❑ the participation of women in local partnerships aimed at promoting social cohesion and such partnerships' impact on equal opportunities issues;

- ❑ the implications of part–time work from a gender perspective;

- ❑ specific gender analyses within projects on ill-health and workplace absenteeism, on work environment and working conditions.

In relation to a wider definition of equal opportunities to encompass factors additional to gender, the Foundation's recent work has included studies on:

- ❑ combating age barriers in job recruitment and training;

- ❑ initiatives and strategies to improve the labour market and workplace integration of people with disabilities;

- ❑ identifying action on the prevention of racism at the workplace, providing examples of good practice and methodologies on how to develop and implement company-level anti-racism programmes.

The Foundation's work has shown the need for complementary strategies at the workplace and in the wider community to build more effective equal opportunities practice. It has sought to clarify the significant role of the social partners and the need to work in partnership with other key actors, including those affected by discrimination and their representatives.

Future orientation

The Foundation will seek to develop further its programme of activities to address equal opportunities, with priority given to gender but also in relation to other bases for direct and indirect discrimination. It will continue, and intensify, its efforts to mainstream equal opportunities issues and to integrate them in all its projects where relevant. The main objectives of its work will be:

❑ to document and evaluate strategies to promote equal opportunities practice in the workplace, in paid and un-paid work and in society in general;

❑ to examine the barriers to, and potential for, improved equal opportunities and increased involvement in decision-making processes for those experiencing direct or indirect discrimination;

❑ to take account of and analyse the impact of major developments, such as the information society, economic and monetary union and the changing nature of the labour market, on equal opportunities between men and women and on other groups subject to discrimination.

Health and well-being

The Challenge

Social progress is not automatically derived from economic growth and development, nor is it equally shared between all citizens. The debate generated by the Green Paper on European Social Policy (COM(93) of 17 November 1993) clearly showed an agreement that social progress must go hand-in-hand with the recovery of economic competitiveness: it is increasingly being recognised that social development is a significant tool in that process. High social standards, which are a complex mix of working and living conditions, are a clear objective of the European Union. High standards of health and well-being are naturally central components of this objective.

The deep-seated changes affecting work and society – such as the ageing of the population and of the workforce; increased economic competition; persistent unemployment; and increased precariousness and exclusion – profoundly influence the health and well-being of the Union's population. Poorer health results in increased costs at the workplace and for society in general, and generates demands for more and improved health care, putting pressure on public services and creating growth in the private sector.

At the same time, the boundaries between life at work and life outside work are becoming blurred, and it is now all the more important to address the challenge of the health and well-being of workers and citizens in an integrated way. While traditional occupational health and safety problems are still on the agenda, the Foundation's work has confirmed that there is an increase in psycho-social (stress), mental health (depression) and musculo-skeletal (RSI) problems. Traditional occupational health policies have their limits. Systems based on regulations, controls and sanctions, focusing on a limited sphere of issues, have to be adapted to new types of jobs and new work situations: such systems may be difficult to apply in smaller organizations or units. Multi-factorial problems, such as stress, have to be addressed in a more holistic way, including life outside work. Strategies for health promotion must be strengthened, particularly if existing inequalities in health and well-being between different groups in society are to be addressed. Global and local pollution is increasingly recognised as having significant health implications, e.g. traffic congestion.

With the establishment of the European Agency for Safety and Health at Work in Bilbao, the Foundation's contribution to meeting the challenge of improving health and well-being will be to develop, more intensively and in new areas, its multidisciplinary, integrated and preventive approach to health and well-being in and outside work.

19

Contribution of the Foundation's past and current programmes

The Foundation has undertaken a considerable body of work under the heading of health and safety over the last eight years. This has been organized around three main areas: the monitoring and assessment of working conditions and health at work; the identification of strategies, policies and instruments with a strong focus on prevention and on health promotion; and an active programme of networking and dissemination with key audiences and with the many organizations working in this field at national and international levels. Amongst the most significant studies have been the following:

- ❏ two surveys on working conditions covering all Member States with analyses in relation to age, gender, sector, occupation, country and company size;

- ❏ the European Health and Safety Database – HASTE;

- ❏ supplementary analyses of working conditions in the EU and by sector, based on existing data and information sources;

- ❏ the development of European networks on product registers and on registers of exposure data;

- ❏ the identification and comparison of various economic incentive systems to stimulate an improved quality of working environment and an analysis of their impacts;

- ❏ assessment of the benefits of stress prevention at the workplace for employees, companies and society and the development of assessment methodology;

- ❏ the development of an integrated approach to the employment of people with disabilities;

- ❏ the documentation and analysis of initiatives to reduce work absenteeism associated with ill-health;

- ❏ the identification and comparative analysis of strategies to promote innovative workplace action for health and the development of associated training programmes;

- ❏ the documentation and assessment of occupational health policies in the Member States.

Health and well-being issues have also been included in a wide range of studies on work organization, working time, environment, social cohesion and equal opportunities.

These studies have been accompanied by a programme of debate and dissemination, including three major European conferences on monitoring the work environment, to stimulate an exchange of information and the development of more coordinated monitoring of health and safety conditions and of more effective instruments and policies.

Future orientation

For its future contribution to this challenge, the Foundation's work will be developed in close collaboration with the Bilbao Agency and in the light of the Commission's proposal for the Fourth Community Programme on Health and Safety at Work, 1996-2000. It will also take account of the extended competence of the EU in public health matters in line with Article 129 (as amended by the Treaty on European Union in 1992) and the contribution its own structure and mandate can bring to an integrated approach to health and well-being issues. Its main objectives will be:

❏ to give priority to a holistic approach based on prevention of risk to health and well-being, with the identification of preventive strategies, instruments and incentives;

❏ to investigate new approaches to improving the quality of life, health and well-being, and to develop new indicators for monitoring and assessment in and outside the workplace, taking into account the changing patterns of work and lifestyles and the demands for an improved environment;

❏ to identify the costs and benefits of measures to promote health at work and in private life;

❏ to assess the quality and effectiveness of public services and utilities which affect health and well-being.

The groundwork for this programme has already been developed. Over the coming years the Foundation will focus particularly on the implications for health and well-being of the changing structure of employment and the content and location of work; the development of the information society; and major social and demographic changes such as changes in family structure, ageing of the population and increasing female participation in the labour market. Health will be examined as an issue in the context of social cohesion and of opportunities for active participation in society. Greater attention will be paid to mental health issues such as stress, depression and coping with change and uncertainty. The development of integrated and multidisciplinary health services and the value of good health as a positive element in economic performance will also be addressed. The further development of activities in this area requires a coordination between the Agency (Bilbao) and the Foundation.

Sustainable development

The Challenge

The Treaty on European Union sets out as one of its principal objectives the achievement of sustainable development. This means developing a policy and strategy for continued economic and social development without detriment to the environment and natural resources, on the quality of which continued human activity and further development depend. As the Brundtland Report[1] stated, this is *"development which meets the needs of the present without compromising the ability of future generations to meet their own needs"*.

Sustainable development requires that wastage and depletion of the world's natural resources should be avoided and optimum re-use and recycling should be encouraged; that there should be a more rational use of existing energy resources and exploration of alternative and environmentally friendly energy sources; and that consumption and behaviour patterns of society should be altered. The move towards sustainable development will continue, supported by action at European, national and local levels. It is likely to be a long process, however, which will require major changes throughout society and hence will affect both the living and working conditions of European citizens. New and more coherent policies, different attitudes and changed organizational structures will be needed, and as sustainable development, eventually, will have to be based on a rather broad consensus in society, new actors will have to be involved in co-operation on its implementation.

Given its structure and close working relationships with the social partners and governments, the Foundation is well placed to contribute to this process. Its main goal will be to identify how the major changes required as part of the move towards sustainable development are likely to affect the quality of life of European citizens. It will aim to point to the adjustments needed and to alternative and innovative solutions to the problems which will arise. This work will be based on analyses of the social, economic and environmental aspects of sustainability, and how to strengthen the positive interaction between them so as to simultaneously achieve European objectives in all three fields.

Contribution of the Foundation's past and current programmes

The Foundation has undertaken a number of activities regarding the socio-economic aspects of sustainable development policies in response to the needs of the EU. These activities include projects on:

❑ new corporate environmental and resource management strategies and the education and training requirements at the different levels of the company;

---

[1] The Report of the World Commission on Environment and Development

22

❑ initiatives aimed at improving the environmental performance of SMEs in southern Europe;

❑ the role and cooperation of the social partners in the environment and their involvement in the process of sustainability, and the introduction of environmental issues in collective bargaining and agreements and in industrial relations in general;

❑ how the implementation of sustainable development policies and measures may affect employment and whether they can be used as a stimulating factor for job creation;

❑ the identification of indicators and good practices for sustainable urban development and how urban innovations, including new concepts and practices regarding urban eco-audits, transport, public spaces and economic revitalization, can contribute to the sustainable city;

❑ the mechanisms, instruments and actions required for a balanced socio-economic and environmental development of medium-sized cities and their regions and the role of these cities in the European urban system;

❑ the testing of existing design methodologies in relation to the design, manufacture and consumption of products in line with the requirements of sustainable development (eco-products).

The focus of this work has been strongly influenced by the structure of the Foundation's Administrative Board, not least the involvement of the social partners, and by the specific competence of the Foundation in the environment area. It has been developed as complementary to the activities of the European Commission and of the European Environment Agency in Copenhagen.

Future orientation

The use of resources and environmental pressures on their use, the introduction of new and more environmentally friendly industrial management and production systems and the development of new kinds of products and patterns of consumption will have a significant impact on European society, on the way industry operates, on employment and thus on living and working conditions and on organizational structures. The Foundation is strongly placed to reflect and develop knowledge on the potential impact of these developments and to stimulate debate at European level on their implications.

The future contribution of the Foundation in this context will have the following objectives:

❑ to identify and assess ways to accelerate action in order to promote awareness and changes in behaviour by industry including, in particular, SMEs and consumers with a view to moving towards sustainable patterns of production and consumption;

23

❏ to investigate and analyse the impact of new instruments and actions in specific sectors, including environmental industries, to balance competitiveness and employment goals with sustainable production and consumption policies and with the improvement of living and working conditions;

❏ to contribute to the development of the concept of shared responsibility and participation by the main social actors (public authorities, public and private enterprises, professional organisations, workers and unions, non-governmental organizations and citizens) in policies and actions to implement sustainable development and to assess their effects.

This work, as before, will be based on the creation and dissemination of knowledge, monitoring and assessing developments and identifying innovative ideas and solutions. A strong emphasis will be placed on the need to develop new education and training schemes and new methods of communication and information for managers, workers and citizens. High priority will be given to ways of improving sectoral and spatial performance relating to the environment and its socio-economic aspects, resource management and eco-efficiency. Special attention will also be paid to the links and interaction between environment and other policies (fiscal, economic, employment, health, safety, social, consumers). The work will continue to be developed in collaboration with the services of the European Commission and in the light of the revised Fifth Programme on Policy and Action in relation to the Environment and Sustainable Development.

Social cohesion

The Challenge

A whole series of European policy statements and documents, from the Treaty of Maastricht itself to the Reports of the Reflection Group and the European Commission on the Inter-Governmental Conference and the Report of the Comité des Sages[2], have emphasised the need to give priority to social cohesion. As the Comité des Sages has said, *"Europe cannot be built on unemployment and social exclusion, nor on an inadequate sense of citizenship. Europe will be a Europe for all, or it will be nothing at all"*.

The dangers of a divided or dual society are clear and already visible. In addition to distress and suffering at the individual and family level, these include social unrest, crime, substance abuse, xenophobia and racial conflict, and greater demands on public resources for income maintenance and social services of all kinds. In contrast a cohesive society, built on values of solidarity, individual and collective rights and responsibilities and active citizenship, lies at the heart of what is known as the European social model and is a key component of economic progress. Increasingly, it is acknowledged that progressive social policies to generate a productive and stable society are required, for reasons both of social justice and economic development.

The pervasive and persistent nature of unemployment, the rapid pace of social, demographic and technological change, the need for competitiveness and the development of economic and monetary union challenge the European Union to bring those who have already become excluded back into the active society, including paid work, and to develop the structures and frameworks to facilitate more cohesive forms of economic and social progress. Issues of basic human and democratic rights, social protection and equal opportunities form crucial foci of attention in this area together with questions of participation, citizenship and self-sufficiency.

The Foundation's contribution will focus on the identification of effective strategies to build a more inclusive and equitable society based on the joint efforts of all the key actors – public authorities, social partners, non-governmental organizations and citizens. In particular, ways to increase the involvement of the marginalized in the development of these strategies will be a specific concern. Reducing the barriers to labour market integration must be a key goal, given the clear links between social exclusion and unemployment and between economic growth and social development.

Contribution of the Foundation's past and current programmes

The Foundation has undertaken many studies relevant to this challenge over the past ten years. The objectives have been to identify

---

[2] Comité des Sages Report: For a Europe of civic and social rights, 1996

practical and successful strategies to reduce the widening gulf between those benefiting from social and economic change and those marginalized and disadvantaged in society. The main questions addressed have been firstly how to increase the involvement of all those concerned in these processes of change, in particular those people and communities affected by exclusion, so that they may themselves contribute to finding solutions.

Secondly, the Foundation has examined ways to improve decision-making and implementation across policy sectors and between different levels of authority. The greater involvement of employers and trade unions in these questions has been a particular focus of analysis.

A range of inter-connected studies has been completed including the following:

- ❑ means to improve social integration and environment in cities, looking at a wide variety of initiatives to promote employment, reduce urban crime, improve transport, housing and environment;
- ❑ the role of public welfare services in combating social exclusion and the development of consumer-oriented initiatives in public services;
- ❑ the strengths and limitations of citizen action in disadvantaged urban neighbourhoods and the need for other key actors to provide a better response to these actions;
- ❑ the role of local partnerships, involving public authorities, social partners and local communities, in combating social exclusion, and analysing the working processes of these as well as their outcomes;
- ❑ the paths of young people towards adulthood and autonomy and how combined housing and employment initiatives can contribute;
- ❑ the improvement of the quality of life for older persons and their carers;
- ❑ the better reconciliation of family and working life, including workers who are carers of older relatives;
- ❑ the improvement of employment opportunities and access to the labour market, especially for the long-term unemployed, older workers and the disabled;
- ❑ the reduction of racism at the workplace and the role of social partners in promoting alternatives to migration.

All these studies have sought to identify more successful strategies and to specify options for improving policy and practice so as to achieve a more inclusive and cohesive society.

▨ Future orientation

Building on the achievements of its past work in this area, the challenge for the Foundation is now to transfer what has been learned by the study of good practice and innovation at the local level to the rethinking of social welfare and social protection systems, including their relationship to employment and the labour market. The main objectives of the Foundation would thus be:

❏ to examine and assess concepts of active citizenship and active social policies and how they are influencing current developments;

❏ to investigate how mainstream public policies can support effective local strategies aimed at building social cohesion;

❏ to look beyond documentation of mechanisms and processes to analyze the real outcomes of innovative developments in policy and practice.

Work has already begun on reviewing new approaches by the social welfare system to tackling social exclusion. The Foundation's 1996 conference on new directions in social welfare will build on and extend this work. New research will aim to identify how Member States can develop and adjust their social welfare and protection systems, bearing in mind issues of finance and accountability. The public sector will form the focus for much of the Foundation's future work on social cohesion, given its key role as an instrument of redistribution and as a guarantor of equality of opportunity and of social justice.

The role of the social partners continues to be significant, especially given the crucial influence of unemployment on the growth of social exclusion, and will be a particular focus of the Foundation's work. Issues such as welfare barriers to economic integration, the relationship between paid and unpaid work, the reconciliation of work and family life, racism, discrimination and the lack of equal opportunities, cannot be tackled without the participation of the social partners alongside the state and citizen.

Key questions to be examined in future work will be how to transfer lessons from successful innovative action to influence the implementation of mainstream policy areas such as social welfare, health and education; how to improve the role of public services in promoting social cohesion, and how to achieve a better balance between work and welfare.

Participation

▨ The Challenge

In a rapidly changing society, increased participation of the main social actors in the decision-making processes and the implementation of policies is an important component of coping with risks and uncertainties. As the Green Paper on European Social Policy pointed out, the combination of the challenges facing the Union must lead to a search for new approaches to responsibility (at the individual and collective levels, in the public and private spheres); new roles for various bodies (social partners, voluntary organizations, public authorities), and new forms of solidarity, leading to new partnerships between all the relevant actors in the field of social policy.

Participation lies at the core of the challenge to promote a more active democratic society. It is also an important tool which can help to reconcile the strengthening of economic performance and competitiveness with the achievement of goals of social solidarity, equal opportunities, sustainable development and a high standard of living and working conditions. The policies needed to address the massive social and structural changes facing the European Union, and the choices these will entail, will require not only more effective implementation of existing mechanisms of participation but also the development of new procedures and processes to involve other key players. A particular challenge is how to improve the involvement of the "grass-roots" – citizens and workers – both for reasons of strengthening transparency and democracy and for developing more effective solutions which can be implemented more efficiently.

The processes of consultation and participation are undergoing review and development, both in the context of working life and in the wider community. The development of information and communication technology offers possibilities to develop new forms of direct and indirect participation to workers, consumers and citizens. Rising levels of education and training also offer more opportunities to react positively to the new demands for information and participation. The emergence of new social actors, of new forms of social responsibility and partnerships, the increasing attention to active citizenship and the contribution of the local community sector to social and environmental issues are key elements affecting the form and content of participation, as is the need to increase effectiveness and efficiency in the use of resources and the performance of public services.

The Foundation has the potential to offer significant support to the understanding of these developments and to the identification of effective strategies and mechanisms to improve processes of consultation and participation. Its goal would be to monitor and analyse new developments so as to identify how increased and more effective participation in many forms and contexts can assist in coping with

28

rapid social and structural change and responding to the challenges facing the Union.

Contribution of the Foundation's past and current programmes

Participation has been one of the central concerns of the Foundation since its creation in the mid 1970s. Given the structure of the Foundation and also the importance of participation as an appropriate means to improve living and working conditions, the role of the social partners and other social actors is obviously central to the Foundation's sphere of interest. The work on aspects of participation has spanned all areas of the Foundation's previous programmes as well as being the subject of a specific series of analyses primarily focused on industrial relations and the workplace.

In relation to the latter, the main areas studied have included the following:

❑ the identification, analysis and dissemination of innovative participatory practices at the workplace, including participation in organizational change, in the introduction of new information technology and in improvements in health and safety;

❑ the evolution of systems of industrial relations and collective bargaining, in particular the development of European employment and industrial relations glossaries and an associated database;

❑ the analysis of the development of new transnational participation practices in companies, specifically participatory structures in European multi-national companies (European works councils);

❑ the preparatory phase of the establishment of a European Industrial Relations Observatory to monitor and analyse trends and developments.

In addition, the following projects have paid particular attention to issues of worker participation, dialogue between the social partners and industrial relations:

❑ the monitoring and analysis of developments in working time organization, including the dissemination of regular bulletins on these issues;

❑ documentation and analysis of company initiatives and collective bargaining on equal opportunities between women and men at work, identifying successful strategies and good practice;

❑ the identification of action to prevent racism at the workplace, providing examples of good practice and how to implement it;

❑ the role and contribution of the social partners to the improvement of the environment.

In its work on improving the quality of life outside the workplace and in developing measures to reconcile working and family life, the Foundation has also paid attention to the issue of participation. It has been a significant focus in the following studies:

- ❏ the role and contribution of local community organisations in responding to social and economic change;
- ❏ the involvement of groups and individuals in the planning, delivery and evaluation of public welfare services;
- ❏ the participation of disadvantaged groups, such as carers and long term unemployed, in the development of initiatives to meet their needs and to re-integrate economically and socially in their communities;
- ❏ the operation of partnerships involving social partners, public authorities and voluntary/community organisations in programmes to promote social cohesion.

Not least the Foundation also contributes to the development of a more active and participative society by itself acting as a forum for debate and active exchange of information and opinion between the key actors in society. It has a major programme of meetings, seminars, summer schools and conferences aimed at involving representatives of European institutions, public authorities, social partners and voluntary/community organisations, not only in a reflection on the main results of its work, but also in the development and implementation of its programmes in all areas of its activities.

Future orientation

It is evident from the above that the issue of participation and the development of a more active society will remain a core focus of the Foundation's work, both in its own right and as an integral element of other studies and of the Foundation's functions. In particular the Foundation will aim:

- ❏ to monitor and evaluate existing and new participatory practices at the workplace in relation to a balanced approach to economic, environmental and social development;
- ❏ to explore innovative approaches (new topics, new forms of co-operation, new partnerships of actors) at different levels and in different contexts in the workplace and in the wider community;
- ❏ to examine the concept of active citizenship, particularly in relation to issues of employment and social protection;
- ❏ to assess the contribution of strategies for user information and involvement in improving the effectiveness and efficiency of public services and in the area of sustainable consumption.

This work will pay attention to the impact of increased labour market flexibility and the continued development of information technology and the globalization of markets and production. It will be closely linked to work focused on equal opportunities and the development of increased social solidarity and cohesion. It will aim to identify the strengths and limitations of different approaches to greater involvement and participation of the various social actors and the instruments, mechanisms and support structures that can support the development of a more participative society. The workplace will continue to be a significant focus for this work with the development of the European Industrial Relations Observatory, which will require careful and prudent implementation so as to build confidence with its different users.

An intensive programme of conferences, seminars and working groups will also be developed to extend the Foundation's role as a forum for debate and discussion. New methods for information, communication and dissemination will be developed to supplement these activities.

CHAPTER 3 Implementing the programme

The activities to be undertaken within this 4 year programme will be developed in detail within the Foundation's annual programmes of work from 1997 to 2000. They will meet the general considerations elaborated at the beginning of Chapter 2 and will be designed to fulfil the orientations as set out within each challenge. Activities will also seek to develop knowledge which will address the six challenges in a transversal way, building an understanding of the relationships and linkages between the major factors of change affecting the quality of living and working conditions in Europe. They will take account in a dynamic way of the areas where the Foundation has an established basis of knowledge, of policy and practice at European and other levels, and of changes in the political and institutional context as they affect the European Union.

The Foundation's areas of expertise

After twenty years' research experience, the Foundation has, in particular, established a considerable base of knowledge in the following areas:

- ❑ **organization of work and the working environment:** conditions associated with the working environment and the organization of working time, as well as conditions associated with the organization of work and labour relations;

- ❑ **industrial relations:** relations between employers and workers in various forms and at different levels: workplace, enterprise, sector, region, country and at European level (social dialogue);

- ❑ **social environment:** related to demographic conditions, but also to the organization of society, family, community, etc. and social protection and welfare structures;

- ❑ **physical environment:** in particular, changes in the natural environment caused by the development of human activities, such as work, industry, transport, leisure, tourism, urbanization;

- ❑ **time:** not only working time but also other uses of time and the interaction between different time schedules in society.

The following table illustrates the kind of relationships which will have to be taken into account in generating and developing the different activities of the Foundation in the coming years.

Areas of expertise Challenges	Organization of work and working environment	Industrial relations	Social environment	Physical environment	Time
1. Employment					
2. Equal opportunities					
3. Health and well-being					
4. Sustainable development					
5. Social cohesion					
6. Participation					

Types of activity

The activities of the Foundation can be grouped into three main types: research and development; debate and discussion; information and dissemination.

Research and development

Research and development concerns the collection, processing and analysis of information, together with the related functions of monitoring and evaluation. With regard to the former, the Foundation's activities may be grouped into two main categories:

❑ surveys and comparative analyses of situations in the Member States (and possibly other countries); such surveys and analyses, if they are to be effectively used in drafting European Union policy, ideally cover all Member States. In the context of the Foundation's programme, the data should facilitate the comparison of living and working conditions across the European Union; such activities are frequently carried out in close collaboration with Eurostat, various observatories and other services of the European Commission (for example, Eurobarometer);

❑ studies aiming to identify and analyse new approaches and innovatory practices as well as the development of pilot projects – activities in principle limited to the countries in which these occur. They can form the basis for exchange and transfer of information and experience.

The aims of the Foundation's research will be to identify and analyse new and existing problems and their causes, to quantify their scale and impact and to search for solutions. Methods may involve surveys, case studies, action research projects, conferences, seminars and workshops, networks, databanks or different combinations of these. Such knowledge is not gathered solely for scientific purposes; it

34

is aimed at leading to conclusions, proposals and/or options which may influence EU policies and programmes. In this perspective, studies must go beyond the analysis of problems to a commitment to finding solutions.

Closely associated with such projects is the need to *monitor* and *evaluate* their progress and outcomes on an ongoing basis. New methods and approaches will be developed so that the Foundation's contribution to confronting the key challenges for European society can be assessed in a way which closely involves the key audiences for its work.

Discussion and debate

Discussion and debate parallel the process of monitoring and evaluation, building opportunities to use the Foundation as a forum where the key social players, on a basis of scientifically produced knowledge and data, can exchange opinions and experience, leading to improved living and working conditions. Such discussion and debate draws on the quadripartite structure of the Administrative Board but also involves other representative organizations and individuals as appropriate. This dialogue between expertise and political expression will increasingly be used to link Foundation work across the key challenges, in elaborating priorities and debating results.

Information and dissemination

Information and dissemination activities are concerned primarily with the widespread mutual exchange, transfer and dissemination of knowledge. They assist in avoiding duplication of work and in achieving complementarity and efficient use of resources. The transfer and dissemination of the results of the Foundation's own research form the main activity within this function: the Foundation already has a range of publications, instruments and services aimed at communicating and actively promoting its work. Increasingly, the Foundation is taking advantage of the opportunities offered by information technology, but the next four years will see an additional emphasis on the improvement of its printed and electronic media products, in line with the new programme approach and the specific needs of its key audiences.

At the same time, the Foundation will continue to develop as an information and reference centre dealing with living and working conditions at European level. It means in particular supplying information and briefings to the European Institutions, Member State governments and the representative organizations of employers and workers. However, there are also a wide range of organizations and individuals interested in the subjects of the Foundation's work, from international to local level, encompassing public authorities, professional organizations, research institutes, voluntary and community organizations, the media and the general public. Appropriate and efficient means to improve the Foundation's information and networking functions will be further developed in the context of its 1997-2000 programme.

European Foundation for the Improvement of Living and Working Conditions

A programme for 1997-2000:
Facing up to the challenges of European society

Luxembourg: Office for Official Publications of the European Communities

1996 – 40 pp. – 21 x 29.7 cm

ISBN 92-827-8593-9

Price (excluding VAT) in Luxembourg: ECU 7